Double Trouble

by June Edelstein
illustrated by Tom McKee

Editorial Offices: Glenview, Illinois • Parsippany, New Jersey • New York, New York
Sales Offices: Needham, Masachusetts • Duluth, Georgia • Glenview, Illinois
Coppell, Texas • Ontario, California • Mesa, Arizona

Every effort has been made to secure permission and provide appropriate credit for photographic material. The publisher deeply regrets any omission and pledges to correct errors called to its attention in subsequent editions.

Unless otherwise acknowledged, all photographs are the property of Scott Foresman, a division of Pearson Education.

ISBN: 0-328-13210-1

Copyright © Pearson Education, Inc.

All Rights Reserved. Printed in the United States of America. This publication is protected by Copyright, and permission should be obtained from the publisher prior to any prohibited reproduction, storage in a retrieval system, or transmission in any form by any means, electronic, mechanical, photocopying, recording, or likewise. For information regarding permission(s), write to: Permissions Department, Scott Foresman, 1900 East Lake Avenue, Glenview, Illinois 60025.

3 4 5 6 7 8 9 10 V010 14 13 12 11 10 09 08 07 06

Peter and Sam were siblings. They weren't just siblings. They were twins. In fact they were not just twins, they were twins who got into a lot of trouble. "Double Trouble" their mother called them.

Now, it's not that they were bad. It's just that trouble followed them around.

"Time to get up," called their mother.

"Breakfast is ready," said their father.

"Mmmphhh," mumbled Peter, not moving.

"Snurrrgle," mumbled Sam, not moving either.

"Time to get up RIGHT NOW!" said their mother firmly. "I don't want you to be late for school."

"If you don't get up right now," said their father, "I am going to eat all of the blueberry pancakes."

The twins loved blueberry pancakes. They got up right away. Maybe it was a little too fast.

Sam got mixed up in his blankets and pillows. The blankets and pillows fell out of the bed. Sam fell off of the ladder.

Peter was already out of bed.

The blankets and pillows fell on Peter. THUNK! Then Sam fell on Peter. THUMP!

Peter fell against the table. The lamp on the table fell to the floor. CRASH!

Sam and Peter's mother looked at the mess. She shook her head. She was not happy.

"Why does this always happen?" she asked. She wasn't really expecting an answer. She got one anyway.

"Sam never thinks about what he is doing," said Peter.

"Peter never thinks about what *he* is doing," said Sam.

"Do too," said Peter. "It's your fault!"

"Do not," said Sam. "It's *your* fault!"

"Remember when our relatives were here for Thanksgiving?" said Peter. "You knocked the turkey right off the plate."

"You should have caught the ball," said Sam. "And what about the time you kicked over that can of paint?"

"You were chasing me," said Peter. "You were jealous because I can run faster. It was your fault!"

"No," said Sam. "It was *your* fault! You do not run faster than I do."

"Hey! That's enough," said their father.

That's what life with the twins was like. There were a lot of messes, and broken things, and arguments about whose fault it was.

Things went on this way until one rainy day when their mother was out shopping. Their father was in the basement fixing Peter's table. The twins didn't know what to do. Then they had an idea about using their skateboards and the chair. It was not a good idea.

The twins built a ramp on the chair. They went down the ramp on their skateboards. They went way too fast.

They fell off of the skateboards! But one skateboard kept going. It kept going until it hit their mother's vase. The vase went CRASH! The twins' father could hear the crash all the way in the basement. He came running upstairs.

"What have you done!" he cried. "That is your mother's favorite vase."

"It was Sam's idea," said Peter.

"It was Peter's idea," said Sam.

"I don't care whose idea it was," said their father. "Just make this better."

The twins were sorry they broke their mother's vase. It would make her sad.

They decided they should earn some money and get the vase fixed. That would be a good surprise.

A new family had just moved in next door. Maybe they needed some help.

"Do you have any work we can do?" asked Sam. "We can rake leaves."

"Hmm," said the neighbor. "I do need some help but not with the leaves. I need someone to play with Tim and Tina while I go upstairs and unpack some boxes."

"Tim and Tina?" asked Peter.

"They are my five-year-old twins," said the neighbor. "Sometimes they get into trouble."

"We can take care of twins," said Sam and Peter.

"You're hired," the neighbor said and went upstairs.

Tim and Tina were kicking a ball in the living room. The ball sailed through the air. It was heading toward the television. Sam caught the ball just in time.

"Kicking a ball in the house is a bad idea," said Peter to Tim and Tina.

"Oh no," said Sam. "Double trouble."
"It was Tim's idea," said Tina.
"It was Tina's idea," said Tim.
The whole afternoon went like that.

Tim and Tina tried to see how many plates they could balance on their heads. Luckily, Peter caught the plates.

Then Tina and Tim tried to see how long it would take to fill the kitchen sink. Luckily, Sam found the mop.

"It is Tim's fault," said Tina every time.

"It is Tina's fault," said Tim every time.

"You are both at fault," said Peter finally.

"Yes," said Sam. "And could you please be a little more careful?"

Then Sam looked at Peter. Peter looked at Sam. They started laughing. "Maybe we can learn from Tina and Tim," said Sam.

"I think so," said Peter.

That evening, Sam and Peter's mother came home from shopping. She saw that the vase was gone and looked at the twins.

"We broke your vase," said Peter. "We were both at fault. We are going to try to be more careful."

"We earned money to fix the vase," said Sam. "We know it is one of your treasures."

"Oh, thank you" said their mother, giving them both a hug. "That vase is a treasure, but you two are my biggest treasures of all."

Twins

There are two kinds of twins. One kind looks alike. They are called identical twins. This kind is always two boys or two girls. The other kind of twins can be two boys, two girls, or a boy and a girl. They may or may not look alike. Many people think that twins have a special relationship.

Stories about twins have been around for a long time. The Navajo Indians have a myth, or story, about twins who free the Earth from monsters. In West Africa, a myth tells about twins, Mawa and Liza, who created the world.

Apollo and Artemis are famous twins from Greek myths. Apollo is the god of light, archery, healing, and music. Artemis is the goddess of the moon, hunting, and giving birth.